JUDITH VON HALL attended school in Ge1 sequently studied architecture. She first encountered anthroposophy in 1997, and began working as a member of staff at Rudolf Steiner House in Berlin, where she also lectured. In addition she had her own architectural practice. In 2004 she received the stigmata, which transformed her life. Her first book was published in German in 2005, and she now works principally as a lecturer and author. She and her husband live in Berlin.

By the same author:

And If He Has Not Been Raised . . .
Descent into the Depths of the Earth
Illness and Healing
The Lord's Prayer
Secrets of the Stations of the Cross

DEMENTIA

Anthroposophical Perspectives

Judith von Halle

With a Foreword by Michaela Glöckler

TEMPLE LODGE

Translated from German by Frank Thomas Smith

Temple Lodge Publishing Ltd.
Hillside House, The Square
Forest Row, RH18 5ES

www.templelodge.com

Published in Great Britain by Temple Lodge Publishing, 2015

Originally published in German in 2010 under the title *Die Demenzerkrankung, Anthroposophische Gesichtspunkte* by Verlag für Anthroposophie, Dornach, Switzerland

© Verlag für Anthroposophie 2010
This translation © Temple Lodge Publishing Ltd. 2015

A CIP catalogue record for this book is available from the British Library

ISBN 978 1 906999 74 2

Cover by Morgan Creative; illustration by freshidea
Typeset by DP Photosetting, Neath, West Glamorgan
Printed and bound by 4edge Limited, Essex, UK

Contents

Foreword

The occasion for the request to write a foreword to this book about dementia was our mutual invitation to the 25th anniversary celebration at the Sonnengarten retirement home in Hombrechtikon, Switzerland. I was curious to know how Judith von Halle, as an engaged anthroposophist, but not a physician, would approach the subject. Furthermore, her perspective as an architect is meaningful for this illness.

Although her descriptions assume a basic knowledge of anthroposophy, it is nevertheless motivating for everyone interested in pursuing the subject, as is done here, to see dementia in a larger, culturally historic context and as an appeal to treat it with spiritualized thinking.

Those involved with this illness professionally or as a relative can learn much from this study, which motivates them to a deepening of anthroposophy. They will also be inspired by how the author brings the illness into the realm of the living impulse of Christ.

Michaela Glöckler
Dornach, 27 October 2009

Preface to First German Edition

This study was the result of a request for an architectural design by an institute caring for people with dementia. Whoever has been in contact with someone affected with dementia or has cared for him or her knows it is symptomatic that such a person is dependent upon a special arrangement of their environment. Because the inner as well as the outer lack of spatial orientation is a fundamental problem, the architectural designer must know the patient's needs well. Such knowledge may be obtained through empirical enquiry. For me, however, it was obvious that the causes of the illness must be investigated before the real needs of the patient can be known, at least to a reasonable extent.

Given that the causes of dementia are unknown to contemporary orthodox medicine, there is reason to investigate which psycho-spiritual factors leading to the outbreak of this illness have not been analysed. The conception of man that is given priority today by the scientific world hardly takes into account that in addition to the physical-material component, for which certain degenerative or pathological processes can be determined with the help of technical apparatus, there are other components of our being to be taken into account which cannot be investigated in that way. So long as the cause of an illness is not sought in connection with those spiritual components of the human being, a successful treatment of the patient cannot be assured.

The design of the patient's living space is of great importance for this treatment. Therefore, it is my opinion that just because of the limitations imposed by spatial orientation, an enormous responsibility is placed on the architect who plans a new living space for the patient. So the task of designing such a living space can only be undertaken on the condition that a previous analysis of the causes of dementia from the perspective of anthroposophical knowledge of humanity be undertaken. The study does not demand medical expertise, but requires an effort to be occupied with the psycho-spiritual conditions under which the dementia patient lives.

Judith von Halle
Dornach, 24 September 2009

Preface to the Second German Edition

On 28 November 2009, shortly after the first edition of this book appeared, a conference on the subject 'Dementia' took place on the occasion of the 25th anniversary of the retirement home Sonnengarten in Hombrechtikon, Switzerland. The organizers asked me to give a talk on that subject based on the fundamentals of my work on dementia. The book on the subject, which had just appeared and included those fundamentals, required advanced knowledge of anthroposophy. But a great part of the public present at the conference, as became apparent, were only marginally or not at all acquainted with anthroposophy, so I was confronted with the task of presenting my ideas in a way that could also be understood by them. After the lecture, not only many of the listeners who had no experience of anthroposophy but also many of the anthroposophists who were present expressed their thanks and considered the lecture to have been more easily understood than the book.

Since the first edition was already sold out after a few weeks and a new one was necessary, I took advantage of the opportunity to respond to the comments I'd received by reformatting the original somewhat and, by means of an introductory chapter, to introduce some basic anthroposophical concepts as well as a number of demonstrative examples.

I hope the readers who had already obtained the

first edition of my book will excuse the fact that an expanded version has now appeared. The contents of the first edition are almost unchanged in the new one. But I hope that the expanded version will be more revealing, also for those who perhaps have not studied anthroposophical spiritual science in depth but are interested in gaining access to an understanding of the causes and the human qualities of dementia.

Judith von Halle
Dornach, 6 January 2010

1. What is the Human Being?

Those who wish to occupy themselves with methods of treating dementia by investigating and acquiring knowledge can achieve positive results without having medical training. One can wonder about this, or doubt it, because dementia is one of the illnesses which are still considered to be incurable and about which orthodox medicine has so far been able to do little to change. This book is meant to show that it is really *necessary* that non-physicians occupy themselves with dementia, and also that the recent proliferation of cases demands a knowledge of the development of our consciousness and the nature of the human being.

Such consciousness about the human being, our true inner and outer nature, can be acquired if we begin to study our own being with the methods of anthroposophical spiritual science. Practising anthroposophical spiritual science is possible for *everyone*. No special qualifications are needed. By being human one is qualified. For it is not at all the task of anthroposophical spiritual science to investigate the spirit, but by means of the spirit to investigate the world and humanity. The fact that this spirit is available to the human being means that we are — without any kind of specialized training — very well equipped for anthroposophical investigative work, provided that we are really willing to do so.

Surely we can advance to higher knowledge with

anthroposophical spiritual science, as is the case with every scientific activity. But anthroposophical spiritual science can be practised by everyone, because it embraces every imaginable field in which one can be interested, and it always begins with what everyone – also those not scientifically trained – can do: *observe*. The precise observation of all the phenomena and events without hasty judgement about what is being observed is the prerequisite for all serious scientific work.

Everyone can practise observing the surrounding objects and events, starting by observing the small, most familiar things, from the processes of growth and decay in a flower to phenomena to which one has not yet been confronted, such as the progression of illness in a dementia patient. Both, the apparently long familiar as well as what has never been seen before, demand close attention from us. For when we quietly observe a long familiar process without the usual hasty evaluation or judgement, we will discover much that we were previously unaware of; it will be like a completely unknown phenomenon.

By means of such exact observation, when we try to curb all the hasty (clever) knowing about what is being observed, suddenly connections will be evident that make clear to us that all observed objects and events are subject to constant change, whether slow or rapid, which, although invisible, does exist and must be permeated with processes and forces. Gradually we come to the certainty that alongside our familiar visible, *earthly* world another, invisible *spiritual* world must exist from which these actions and forces emanate – as for example the stimulus which lets the plant grow and decay, or that invisible but undeniably real intense feeling of love, or of loathing.

Only by carrying out such simple but earnest observation exercises will we recognize this spiritual world as omnipresent, for it is what permeates our material, visible outer world. And we will recognize that everything we perceive of the external world with our sensory organs is vivified by it.

Therefore, anthroposophical spiritual science takes on the task of first observing the essence of the world and of the human being just as they are, namely in their outer nature and their inner spiritual relationships, and then to fathom them. Anthroposophical spiritual science investigates the same things as does natural science, only not in a 'test tube', but by means of refined spiritual perception.

For an in-depth investigation of the relationships between the outer world and the spiritual world, however, other organs of perception than the sensory ones are needed. Simple exercises, such as the already mentioned observation exercise, lead to the gradual training of such supersensible organs through what takes place in the soul by means of pure observation.[1] It is worth mentioning that the development of supersensible organs, according to equally clear rules, occurs as does the development of sensory organs. The disclosures resulting from the use of supersensible organs are also to be compared with each other as are the results and disclosures which we make through the use of our sensory organs. Just as two rational persons would not argue as to whether the sky as a rule is blue and not green, so would two persons with supersensible organs not argue about whether there are body-free, living beings in the supersensible world, to which human beings also belong when they are body-free in the time between death and a new birth and are living in the spiritual world.

When we consider the human being from the anthroposophical point of view, a certain discrepancy arises with the approach of many natural scientists; for anthroposophical spiritual science contemplates the human being as a *spiritual* being. This spiritual being has its home in the spiritual world and unites itself, through incarnation, with the physical body, which serves as an instrument to live in the physical–material world and to work in it, beginning in the womb after conception. Therefore the human being is a part of this spiritual world and remains so after he is born. We can say that the earthly human being is at least as much a spiritual being as a physical one; in reality the ratio is three to one. For whoever investigates and describes the human being in a spiritual-scientific way will come to the conclusion that he consists of four different components of being, only one of which is the physical–material body that we see in the mirror.

At first we have the familiar material, physical body that we can feel and touch. It contains our organs, which can degenerate when affected by an illness and may be treated by means of surgery. Only this material body has taken on the same characteristics as the mineral kingdom. It is matter which, had it not been permeated with something completely different, would be as rigid and lifeless as a stone. But the human being possesses besides this physical body one which in anthroposophical spiritual science is called the 'life body' or 'etheric body'. This body, invisible to the sensory organs, works as a spiritual, vivifying force into the organs of the physical body and makes them functional. We possess this life body, or etheric body, in common with the vegetable kingdom. Plants also have a material body which we can touch as we do a stone, but they grow and bloom and then wither. A force of an 'etheric' nature acts in them, which vivifies the dead material. But the human being has, in addition to the physical and etheric bodies, another component of his being, namely what we usually call the 'soul'. This component, which in anthroposophical terminology is called the 'astral body', basically works in the nervous system, bringing forth the feelings which we sense within us and which we all too often allow to lead us. With this component we stand at the stage of the animal kingdom. Animals, in contrast to plants, have the astral body as their highest component. They have feelings which they can express. But finally the human being possesses a fourth element, which raises him above the animal kingdom: it is the 'I'.[2] Through the I, the human being has a clear consciousness of self; he is able to apprehend himself and the world in thought. One can also call this I the 'spirit'. We are concerned with this spirit when we grapple with dementia, because the word dementia includes the word spirit (*mens*).

Physical body	visible
Etheric body	
Astral body	invisible, spiritual components
The I	

Medical science today is feverishly occupied with seeking a treatment for dementia and also for its causes. Admittedly some small successes have been achieved with the discovery of means which delay the degenerative process of dementia. But in fact, with the help of conventional medicinal and natural-scientific procedures, we have neither discovered exactly what triggers this illness nor how it can be treated. The degenerative processes are studied, but even when the material processes can be exactly described the question of 'why' remains. Incidentally, this also applies to most illnesses, above all the incurable ones. Why does a cell degenerate and cancer develop? Of course there are risk factors, but people die of cancer although none of the risk factors apply to them. Why does one person catch influenza when another, who had the same close contacts, does not? Why does it break out in one person on a certain day and not in another? The 'hardline' natural scientists would answer that this depends upon certain material pre-conditions. But then we could again ask: Why do such preconditions apply on that particular day?

In respect to such questions about the 'why', we might remember a typical scene in physics class during our schooldays when the revolutions of the planets around the sun were explained using objects floating in water that are put in motion using a stick or a spoon. That depiction of centrifugal force can appear to be very illuminating, but who, some naive (in the best sense) pupils might be inclined to ask, is responsible for the impulse in planetary space. Who holds the stick or the spoon? Many teachers point to the so-called big bang, and pupils may prefer to be silent when the question arises in them again: Who is responsible for the big bang? Therefore it isn't strange that the greatest natural scientists, above all physicists, finally reach for the concept of God. This concept of God is only revealed when one recognizes the invisible *spirit* as the cause of material phenomena.

Whoever arrives at an enhanced and accurate envisioning of the human being such as spiritual science makes possible will quickly see the plausibility of also keeping the spiritual relationships in mind when evaluating physical phenomena. It has been shown that scientists who believe the human being to be the product of a 'randomly determined gene-lottery',[3] instead of psycho-spiritual in nature, and regard material degeneration as being caused by randomness, can hardly arrive at the causes of illnesses such as dementia. If the spiritual components of the person are not taken into consideration, finding the causes of illness is hardly imaginable; one can only treat the symptoms, which does not lead to a cure. Many orthodox methods, based on a distorted image of man, only achieve a *suppression* of the symptoms. This word is appropriate for the process that takes place in the patient when he is treated with such means. For in fact what the illness wants to express is sup*pressed*, pressed downward. The essence of the illness, its cause, also its spiritual reason and purpose, instead of being treated is forced down into the deeper layers of the human being, and the destiny or karma which should have been fulfilled by this illness is pushed forward to a later point in time, perhaps even to a future incarnation. Naturally such a suppressed illness will find expression at the next opportunity in a much more severe way.

Recognition of the spirit in the human being and the universe is, however, quite difficult for our contemporary culture. Whoever speaks of such things will often only be laughed at by the wise men of science. In this respect there is a simple, everyday observable example to show how the spirit vivifies matter and that matter could never exist without the spirit: it is death. With nothing else can the real impulse of the spirit be so graphically illustrated. Every day someone in our direct proximity abandons his or her physical body. Whoever has stood at a deathbed will have witnessed this great moment: the human being whom we knew abandons his bodily dwelling. Here it becomes very clear to us that we had not loved the physical person, but that the physical body of this person was really only the earthly appearance that the real person had assumed; and now the mere physical component lies in the deathbed, but it is no longer the true human being. The true human being, namely the spiritual one, has gone to another place, to another world in which he needs no physical body. Basically, everyone should be able to understand this: when the person's spirit is present in the physical body it permeates it, works in it so that the physical body can walk around. If the spirit is removed from the physical instrument, it lies unmoving and rigid.

We can make a similar observation with a sleeping person. When asleep the spirit and the soul, that is, the I and the astral body, leave the physical body and move to the spiritual world. The life body, however, remains united with the physical component, for the organic functions remain unaffected during sleep. Nevertheless, when the person's spirit is in the spiritual world while sleeping he cannot move around, he only lies in bed. As soon as the spirit is brought back again into the physical component he can again rise and guide his limbs around the room. When the human being passes through the gates of death, his spirit does not return to the bodily component. But he does not disappear. He lives in his true spiritual home, until one day he returns in a new incarnation and acquires a new physical body. This thought explains the secret of the Christ-impulse. 'I am the resurrection and the life,' Christ tells Martha.[4] Christ is the 'I AM', which is given to each of us. This I, the fourth component of being, is the spiritual in man; it is our actual individuality. And this actual individuality is not decomposable—it is immortal. Consequently the I is the 'resurrection', for it overcomes death in that it rises out of the decomposing material body and enters its spiritual home undamaged, and that is 'the life'.

Therefore the human being is a spiritual being who during his earthly sojourn resides in a material body, which has been built by higher spiritual beings.[5] When one regards man as the being which he really is, namely consisting of four different components, it is then possible to speak anthropologically about this being, even if one has completed no medical studies. By means of anthroposophical spiritual science, for example, knowledge of the physical nature of the human being can be acquired without dissecting his body.

By means of the example of the sleeping state, we can observe that man's components of being can pass through various stages so that the whole person is 'mobile'. Also in the case of an illness the various human components are in movement; something exceptional is happening to him. If we recognize that the human being is permeated and thereby strengthened with spiritual impulses, then we have achieved a real scientific contribution to the knowledge of man. On the other hand, we can understand why orthodox medicine, despite all its achievements contributing to human well-being, does not advance in many aspects and is unable to answer many questions about the causes of illnesses. But if we approach the true causes of illnesses, in many cases treatment would not have to remain at the stage of treating symptoms.

Given that man is a *spiritual* being with a physical body, it is obvious that the causes of an illness are not to be found in the physical context, but rather the physical breakdown is recognized as the impulse of spiritual causes and these causes are to be sought within the spiritual components of the human being.

2. The Origin of Remembrances and their Recording in Memory

If one strives for a treatment for dementia that involves finding the causes and not the symptoms, an accurate as possible picture of the direct relationship between the physical and the spiritual composition of the human being should be attained, starting with how he appears in his normal state.[6] By comparing then the divergences from the normal state as they arise when dementia occurs, we can also discover clues about the causes.

One of the first symptoms of the dementia phenomenon is the diminishing remembering capacity of the affected person. But what are remembrances anyway? How do they arise? Remembrances are representations (mental pictures) that we register in our memory, which is in our etheric body. To be precise, we should call them memory-representations, because our remembrances as a rule never show what actually took place. Something happens, we have a sensory perception of a scene, then we immediately form representations about this sensory perception. In reality we never remember the exact sensory perception, but only our representation, or mental picture, of the sensory perception. We file this representation in our memory until we retrieve it again as a remembrance. The astral body does the retrieving. Speaking metaphorically, it reaches down into the etheric body and takes out the filed representation from our memory and brings it into consciousness. When external facts correct us, we realize that our remembrances are related to our representations and are thus only more or less precise. For example, you remember the distribution of the rooms in a building you once entered. When you re-enter the building, you realize that it is different from what you remembered. It is also the case with respect to times and places, or remembering people's faces.

There are two kinds of memory-representations: those related to exterior events, that is, the remembrance of representations we have made of sensory perceptions, and those of a psychic nature unrelated to exterior sensory perceptions—what we could call abstract ideas.

These two kinds of representations are recorded with different speeds and in different 'places' in our memory. The representations that have a purely psychic origin and are not the result of direct I-activity—when sensory perceptions are involved, for example—as a rule are impressed into the etheric body in a shorter time than are later recallable memories; whereas remembrances of external events require substantially longer to be firmly impressed in the etheric body. This process of recording at differing speeds, according to the kind of representation, is a process that is executed unconsciously and is invisible to our outer senses. The differing speeds of the recordings depend on how deeply the representation has been impressed in the etheric body. In contrast to the representations that are rapidly transferred to the etheric body (those not directly related to a sensory perception and remain, metaphorically speaking, in the 'upper' layers of the etheric body), the memory-representations of exterior events are rooted in the 'deeper' layers of the etheric body.[7] There, embedded in the etheric body's memory, the representations are stored like the yearly rings in the trunk of a tree, so that the representations of events experienced a long time ago are, as a rule, harder to retrieve and bring to consciousness than those formed a short time ago. According to whether the memory-representations are stored in the upper layers of the etheric body (in the outer yearly rings of the tree-trunk, so to speak) or in the inner layers we can regard them as short-term and long-term memories.

Although remembrances of sensory perceptions take longer to be recorded, for the same reason they sink deeper into memory and are thus made more lasting. Remembrances of the psycho-spiritual, of abstract ideas, are stored more quickly in memory, and therefore less deeply. In the less deep-lying, short-term memory, mostly abstract psycho-spiritual memory-representations are recorded; whereas in the deeper-lying, long-term memory, mostly remembrances of concrete events are recorded. This means that as a rule we can remember, although it is perhaps more strenuous, concrete events of the past longer than our past mental pictures, or representations, which are not related to thoughts about the outer world.

Thus the inner development of the memories found in the etheric body can be imagined as follows: the remembrances of long-ago sensory impressions are found in the inner core of the 'tree-trunk'; then, over them, are the remembrances resulting from sensory impressions; and again over them, or alternating with them, in the outer layers of the 'trunk' (depending on whether they arose in childhood or in early or late adulthood) those representations which did *not* originate from outer sensory perceptions.

Of course these recordings constitute a continuous process, so representations of events having taken place in the outer sensory world can at first also be found in the short-term memory region. These, however, 'sink' deeper into the etheric body over time.

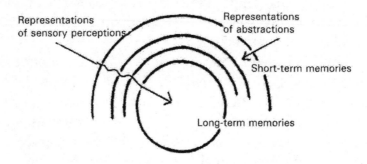

Representations of sensory perceptions

Representations of abstractions

Short-term memories

Long-term memories

Therefore it is important to distinguish the various components and their tasks and activities if we wish to understand the origin of a remembrance. The I-consciousness is attached to the sensory perceptions of the exterior world. The representations, however, are bound to the astral body. Most events that belong to the so-called short-term memory, that is, the ones impressed in the 'upper' layer of the etheric body, are bound with the events and perceptions that are *not* associated with exterior events and representations. However, every representation arising from a sensory perception, as already mentioned, is to be found at first in the short-term memory region before it is permeated with the long-term memory—in other words, before it sinks down into the 'lower' layers of the etheric body and disappears within the inner rings of the 'tree-trunk' (because it is overlain by newer ones).

Only when 'the I is turned into a mirroring device'[8] of the soul for the events and impressions that permeate the human being from the outer world — which occurs at first during childhood — is it possible to remember anything. But the quality of the remembrance is always variable depending on the kind of representation. We can observe in ourselves that there are very few representations made during childhood that do *not* come from the content of the exterior sensory world and then recorded in our long-term memory. Mostly they are very impressionable remembrances, which indicates that in childhood only rarely does a conscious I-activity in relation to the representations occur, and when it does it differs sharply from the sensory impressions which the child otherwise receives. Such sensory-free representations recorded in the long-term memory consist mostly of psycho-spiritual experiences, the investigation of which requires the forces of the consciousness soul.

When the I makes the representations that are connected to the activity of the astral body fully conscious, it can be compared to a meditation process — which leads to the recording of representations that are not bound to the senses in the long-term memory of the etheric body.[9]

Representations from childhood that are *not* made conscious also permeate the etheric body, but one cannot say that they, like the others, belong to the long-term memory, because they are not remembered, that is, they cannot be recalled from the long-term memory. They continue to rumble around in the etheric body and cause disturbances, which result in illnesses in the soul as well as in the physical body. When the I is weakened, which as a rule causes the lower components of being to be unrestrained and uncontrolled thereby strengthening them, these disturbances can, in some cases, erupt violently.[10]

Of course not only representations of outer events, which we have received through our sensory perceptions, are deposited in the long-term memory. Also remembrances of abstract ideas and feelings that have not arisen by means of sensory events are recorded in the long-term memory. This can happen, for example, when a person remembers an idea which is in agreement with spiritual reality and is not a mere 'dead' cobweb of thoughts, as Rudolf Steiner called it. It can also happen that at the moment of his representation he is conscious of its potential subjectivity. Something like this—as indicated above—can be achieved through meditation, in which one learns to observe one's own ideas as the expressions of another person. This observing with our spiritual senses happens with a precision at least as great as when we observe outer events with our bodily senses. The person can bring his representations to consciousness during meditation, by observing the astral body with his I, so to speak. Therefore, meditation or regular retrospection[*] allows representations to be integrated

---

[*]Retrospection (*Rückschau*): a meditative exercise recommended by Rudolf Steiner whereby before going to sleep one reviews the day in reverse, from end to beginning. (Trans.)

into what Rudolf Steiner called the 'remembrance-tableau' of the etheric body.[11] (The conscious forming of the etheric body through sorting of sensory-free representations that are still bound to astral urges and desires, and the memory-representations of sensory perceptions, help to form the so-called Life Spirit—the etheric body spiritualized by the I.)

We are able to embed the abstract representations in long-term memory more rapidly and successfully when we have worked on those representations with the I, that is, when we have brought our representations (mental images or ideas) clearly to consciousness. This can also be done by means of nightly retrospection, in which we clean out the astral body of all kinds of worthless representations that have accumulated during the day. This method is a very good means of avoiding memory loss. We could also say that it is a good means of preventing representations being stored only in short-term memory, where much that is stored does not penetrate to the inner layers of long-term memory, but only remains for a 'short' time in memory and then vanishes. Sorting of remembrance-representations during the evening retrospection helps to banish the petty and super-fluous to short-term memory, whereas the meaningful is consciously cultivated and thus transferred to long-term memory.

An example of how memory deals with abstract representations can lead us back to schooldays. Possibly we have all pondered the question of whether we should simply memorize a mathematical formula or try to really understand it. Once we have bitten through the hard crust and have made the abstract formula our own through the force of conscious thinking, we will also be able to use it for many years into the future. It is different if we decide not to learn it for a lifetime, but only to pass the examination. We memorize something and file it in short-term memory, where it mostly only lasts until the unavoidable exam has been passed. Years later we may not even remember that we ever used such a formula. The consciousness of abstract representations and thoughts is therefore a quite reliable means of keeping track of them and being able to retrieve them again from memory. By regularly practising a meditative retrospection one is protecting the remembrance-representations and working on our astral body, in which feelings proliferate, and on the etheric body, in which habits are rooted, in a hygienic way.[12] And even if one day we suffer from a loss of memory, we will benefit by our etheric and astral bodies having been treated hygienically; we might even have unique spiritual experiences, because we have liberated ourselves from 'mechanical thinking'.[13]

The decline of physical expression in the head-organization, as it appears in advanced dementia when disintegrated brain cells are apparent, is a pathologically accelerated evolution of humanity in general, caused by certain spiritual powers. It is a fact that the human being has always evolved since his appearance on earth. There has never been a stand-still. The human body stood at the height of its development during the ancient Graecian epoch. The artistic ideal of Graecian beauty is witness to this.

But the Christ-event was a turning point of time for the earth as well as for human evolution. Not only the earth itself, but also the physical-material nature of man as a constituent part of earthly matter has been in a gradual process of degeneration since then. Something else must therefore step forward to take the place of the gradually declining physical body if humanity is to continue inhabiting the earth. This degradation of humanity's material nature also provides the opportunity to put something else in its place. What must take the place of the decayed material nature is a spiritualized physical corporeality. And if during this process of decay the brain also degenerates little by little, it is clear that the thought process must also be gradually transformed. Intellectual brain-thinking, which at some point will no longer be possible because the organ has atrophied, would have to be replaced by a spiritualized thought process. But this will only be possible with a strong I devoted to spiritual impulses, for example through a spiritual, not merely intellectual, thought training.

That ever more people in western culture are stuck in the decay of their material nature is because they do not fill the gaps left by the physical decline in the fabric of their being with such spiritual thinking. This means that the decline of material nature—for example the dying of brain cells—would not necessarily be a problem provided that the human being has developed in a timely fashion something capable of taking their place. This was the purpose of the Mystery of Golgotha, to bring the human being to a stage equal to that of the Resurrected One on Easter morning, that is, to create a non-decomposable physical body through his I-forces—a no longer mineral-physical, but a spiritualized physical body.

3. The Difference Between 'Normal' Forgetfulness in Old Age and Dementia

In dementia the loss of short-term memory is noticed first. This means that in the etheric body there is an excess of stored representations, or rather memory-representations, that have not been processed by the I.

In other words, the failure of short-term memory does not mean that there are no more remembrances in it. On the contrary, if we observe with spiritual eyes a person who is losing his short-term memory, perceiving his aura, so to speak, we will note that short-term memory loss occurs when he has accumulated too many remembrances. Imagine a picture of a fragile pot into which ever more amounts of grain, stones or something similar are poured until it is completely full. If you continue trying to pour things into it, the new things will simply fall over the rim, that is, will not be contained. Or, if you try to force new things in, the pot will burst and everything in it will pour out and be lost.

If this begins to happen, the attempt can be made to compensate for the excess weight in short-term memory by therapeutically transferring the old representations to consciousness, that is, by remembering and consciously processing them—in a kind of retrospection. It is fascinating to observe that the human being, who is brilliant in his subconscious because in his higher being higher spiritual forces are at work, intuitively uses therapy on himself. As soon as he experiences an increase in forgetfulness in the short-term memory area, he begins on his own to remove old remembrances from his long-term memory in order to compensate for the excess of unclear short-term memories or almost completely empty short-term memories. Encouraged, he begins to talk about his old experiences.

This is a *completely normal* process. Many people of advanced age who suffer from a certain loss of short-term memory and notice or are informed that they often talk about childhood experiences, fear that they have dementia. Also relatives who have heard that the difficult process of dementia starts with such a symptom are alarmed and often get panicky. Even doctors find it difficult to distinguish real dementia in its early stage from 'normal' *old age forgetfulness*. Many elderly people live in fear and anxiety about being affected themselves and know no peace.

The loss of short-term memory and the strengthened retrieving of remembrances from long-term memory in ageing people are processes which are normal and even healthy, as the observation of human nature using anthroposophical methods shows. This can easily be explained.

The 'normal' forgetfulness of old age is, as a rule, a sign — parallel to the steadily advancing decline of the physical body — that the etheric body has begun to gradually expand, something that invariably happens towards the end of a spiritually enriched life. It can begin to gradually occur at around 72 years of age.[14] By then the individual has mostly experienced and realized the great impulses of life. New impressions are no longer received and processed as they were before this time; rather the person begins to prepare for crossing the threshold and carries out a retrospection of what has been done, felt and thought during his earthly life. In fact, the incessant reception of new impressions hinders the process of preparation for crossing the threshold and the retrospection of his life.

Experience shows that older people can very well absorb the events and concerns that are important to them. Only they separate — as a matter of course — the important from the less important, which they soon forget. In most cases this is not really harmful. This process leads to the admirable composure of older people. Much of what young people erratically accept and which they consider terribly and urgently important, and which quickly excites them, is less important for an older person. He considers the erratic behaviour of youth to be a 'tempest in a teapot', and often he is quite correct. Perhaps this is a bit of the 'old age wisdom' of human nature, which insures that in old age the many everyday impressions that flood into us are pushed back and reduced to the essential, whereas at the same time the reviewing and processing of older memories leads to conclusions and learning which are not accessible to a younger person.

What happens, though, when remembrances are extracted from the long-term memory? By extracting the old impressions stored in the etheric body, which once formed and permeated a person's life, his etheric body *expands*, a process which is concluded at death, that is, with the permanent separation of the etheric body from the physical body. This expanding of the etheric body is accompanied by a characteristic phenomenon in which, in the case of a 'healthy' normal ageing-related forgetfulness, the etheric body becomes 'thinner' as it continuously expands. (Because most of the words in our language describe the exterior nature surrounding us, it is not easy to find the right concepts for this process. One could also say that the etheric body becomes 'spiritually finer'.) Everyone who perceives with some sensibility will realize that an older person's etheric body becomes more delicate. When young people are forgetful, the same process underlies the phenomenon, namely the expansion of the etheric body. However, this process should not take place in early years. But we must also say that the etheric body 'dilutes' in such a case.[15] However, with forgetfulness in youth we should rather state that forgetfulness is related to a *weakening* of the etheric body. This is described in anthroposophical terminology as 'luciferic', because it is trying to avoid the sensory bound perceptions, that is to say, the recording of mental pictures of these perceptions in the deeper components of the individual.

Dementia is also accompanied by an enlargement of the astral body. But there is a considerable difference between this and normal old age forgetfulness, which, among other things, is attributable to the slow *detachment* of the etheric body. (There is also a difference in the youthful weakening of the etheric body when there is forgetfulness.) In dementia the opposite occurs: the expanding etheric body is *hardened* by the unprocessed recordings it contains. It is to be noted that now the I, the highest component of being, which is described above as the 'spirit', is withdrawing from the organization of the other components of being. Because of this withdrawal of the I, which in effect impels and accounts for the illness, the extracted long-term remembrances can no longer be firmly processed. Instead they force themselves up into the already overfull short-term memory, until the enormous accumulation of memory-representations, unprocessed by the I, cause an etheric hardening. This hardening can even advance to the physical.[16] The etheric body swells with this hardening, instead of thinning. This causes it to have difficulty separating from the physical body. The person then has great trouble dying quickly and harmoniously.

In dementia two factors meet. In one there is a gradual loss of short-term memory. An autodidactic attempt to make old remembrances or representations conscious takes place in order to reduce the preponderance of unprocessed memory-representations so that new perceptions and representations may again be integrated. If this happens with the partial or complete absence of the I, however, the process takes place unconsciously.

The person is then (until the later complete loss of memory) increasingly only able to remember what happened long ago. But he begins – instead of consciously processing the old representations and events – to live so firmly in the past that everyday tasks can no longer be mastered, and new perceptions and representations are suppressed, and finally the essentials of everyday life can no longer be assimilated. The etheric body is no longer vitalized by the conscious processing and integrating of new impressions, so it hardens and this hardening causes an enormous overweight for the higher components of being: the astral body and the withdrawing I. This process takes place through the impulses of the so-called 'ahrimanic' beings.

4. The Trinitarian Impulse of Spiritual Forces in Human Beings and in the World

Now for a glance at a subject which may be self-evident to those familiar with anthroposophy, but which is hardly noticed by a large segment of contemporary culture. It concerns the impulses of spiritual beings, real entities which, however, must be perceived otherwise than with mere physical eyes, but which can be perceived in others as well as in one's self by some reflection. A reference to these already-mentioned beings is necessary here, because they are directly involved in the causes of dementia, despite their existence usually being denied.

If we recognize the existence and force of our I, our highest component of being, then the question may arise: Are there also spiritual forces which are opposed to the I? And this question, if considered calmly from a more elevated point of view or in a nightly retrospection, can be answered with 'yes'. There are indeed spiritual forces that are combating the impulses and the activities of the I and who want to impose their own impulses in the place of the human being's. By means of such a self-observation process, one can abandon the unhealthy idea of dividing the world into good and evil, into heaven and hell, that is, a *duality*. The human being of today has developed sufficient strength of consciousness to perceive the impulses of two spiritual beings in himself, and in others, which are opposed to the Christ-impulse, that is, to our I-activity. What these beings are called is basically unimportant. Here we will use the designations known and utilized for centuries in esotericism: 'Lucifer' and 'Ahriman'.

Much could be said about both of these opposing powers, but here a brief characterization will suffice. The principal characteristic of the luciferic powers is the tendency to wrench the spiritual in man from the earthly material element. The goal of these luciferic powers is to alienate man from his earthly dwelling, to make him turn away from his earthly works and life. For them the psycho-spiritual in the human being should not be united or remain with the incarnated earthly man, with his bodily housing, which constitutes, after all, an instrument for the spiritual man. If the psycho-spiritual of the human being cannot make use of this instrument, it strives to abandon the earth and does not want to fulfil its true tasks during this incarnation: to be engaged in earthly works and in the earth's evolution. The manifest consequence of a luciferic influence in human soul-life is not only egotism and unworldliness, the involvement in 'religious' fantasies, or rather religious fanaticism, the gawking at 'nirvana'; the luciferic impulse is also manifest in today's well-known submission to abstract thoughts and lofty intellectualism. Given that the luciferic resides in the spheres in which we suppose 'heaven' to be, it is often fatally confused with the good divine beings, with 'heaven' itself. The human being, who is accustomed to think of the duality of 'heaven' and 'hell', strives to escape from hell, namely from Ahriman, and in this way lands directly into the jaws of Lucifer – if he doesn't realize that it is not Christ but Lucifer who stands opposed to Ahriman, or that the universal being and the human being are permeated by a *trinity* rather than a duality.

The second spiritual power opposing the human I is the ahrimanic being, which acts in direct opposition to the luciferic impulses. It tries to subject the spiritual in humanity to matter. The psycho-spiritual is meant to be subjected so much to the laws of the earth, of matter, that it denies *itself*. Ahrimanic influence in the human soul is recognizable in the greed for ownership, but also in doubting spiritual reality. In our times the ahrimanic influence has advanced so far that it denies our spirit and claims that the human being is nothing more than the result of a 'randomly determined gene-lottery'. Therefore man is not responsible for any of his actions; because if he does not possess an I, and all his thinking, feeling and acting are determined by matter, by genes, he cannot be held responsible for any of his immoral acts. Due to this scientific theory, a change in juridical opinion is already being considered. Ahriman—himself a *spiritual* being—has managed to convince man that there are no spiritual beings, and therefore he himself is not one (the perfect basis for uncontrolled behaviour). Whoever accepts the reality of an ahrimanic influence today is laughed at by those who prepare the field for Ahriman by claiming that he doesn't exist. Those people, who feel superior because of such thoughts, are the ideal tools for the ahrimanic powers.

It is notable that humanity had always known about the existence of spiritual powers and it is only in the past century that an about-face from this obvious fact has taken place—an about-face that is so radical that it isn't even shaken by the spiritual history of humanity, which speaks a different language, and instead believes itself to be at the peak of enlightenment. To verify these divergent forces through the empirical observation of one's self is basically quite easy and requires no degree in literature but at most a little good will and reasoning. Every person can experience in himself how the polarizing forces of Lucifer and Ahriman wrench and rend, causing him to quarrel internally with himself and the world. If he does not try to balance these forces he rapidly loses his centre, his inner equilibrium. The central force which makes this balance possible is the Christ-impulse, that of his I. The Christ-force of the I stands as a balancing force between the polarities of the opposing forces, which above all want to take possession of our lower components: the astral body and the etheric body. Thus the human being lives in a trinitarian relationship. By not recognizing this trinity, he is continually exposed to the danger of being pulled back and forth between the duality of Lucifer and Ahriman and is not able to find his own divinity.

By following the influences of Lucifer and Ahriman from an overall perspective as they relate to humanity's cultural history, we find these influences in the various territories and cultures of the earth. It is obvious that the luciferic influence is greater in India, and in Asia as a whole, whereas on the other side of the ocean, in the American countries, the ahrimanic influence holds sway. (Here the impulses which originate out of the eastern and western regions *themselves* are meant.) It should not be forgotten, however, that through these influences great advances have been made in the world, which are indispensable for our human development. Therefore the implementation of technical achievements, for example, is not ahrimanic *per se*. It only depends on whether these achievements of the western world are used for humanity's beneficial evolution in a way that the I, our highest component of being, is always master of the systems. It would be self-deceiving to believe that by strictly avoiding all the many influences which pervade our lives, such as television, internet or mobile phones, we can escape from them. Even if you give up the car, at some point you will have to board a train or switch on the heat or electric light, use a refrigerator or a washing machine. Also, practically all people enjoy food, which — even when it bears an 'organic' label — would never have landed on the plate without the achievements of western culture, whether it involves a tractor, a milking machine or logistical management know-how, including transport from producer to retailer. Whoever tries in this way to flee from Ahriman's influence is on a sure path to a world ruled by Lucifer.

On the other hand, we should not be unappreciative of the 'blessings' of the eastern world. Whoever is no longer able to descend into himself, to recognize and heed the world of soul and spirit and not be ashamed to let an honest religious — not confessional — feeling flow into him, will, in the long run, not be able to avoid the influence of the ahrimanic powers.

Only if, with respect to these differing influences, no balancing forces intervene which supplement each of these principles with the other and thereby

eliminate the preponderance of one of them, culturally as well as territorially, only if these forces do *not*
intervene does a polarization of cultures result.

Rudolf Steiner indicated that the human being of
the west today, in contrast to oriental cultures of the
past, does not formulate perceptions and representations by means of the so-called higher senses, but
predominantly by means of the lower of the twelve
senses (sense of smell, sense of taste, sense of balance,
sense of movement, sense of life and sense of touch).
This has become a peculiarity of western culture,
which deals with the analytically scientific conception
of the world, more with the material aspect and less
with the spiritual aspect.[17] Thus a malformation of
western culture is manifested, namely in materialism,
due to the prevailing use of the lower senses; this is an
ahrimanic impulse. The degeneration of the eastern
world-view due to the prevailing use of the higher
senses is manifested in unworldliness, in the concentration of ideas about liberation from matter; this is
a luciferic impulse.

Thus both tendencies—when each stands for itself
alone—lack the mediating force of the Christ-impulse.
The healing balance of both tendencies is the secret of
the Christ-mystery, through which the spirit is united
with matter (the otherwise upward striving luciferic
principle unites itself with the earthly depths) and
matter with the spirit (the otherwise downward
striving ahrimanic principle unites itself with the
heavenly heights).

When we observe the cultural landscape of our
earth, we realize that Europe is not only territorially in
the middle between the above-mentioned regions;

Europe could also be the culturally historic mediating force of the Christ-impulse, which binds together the most beneficial of the western world and the most beneficial of the eastern world. To represent the Christ-impulse in the rest of the world and have it stream into it should be the task of all of central Europe.

But has Europe seized upon this task? Doesn't Europe tend towards one of the dual cultural impulses? We could hardly deny that Europe's self-reliance, which could and should become that mediating force, has dissolved more and more. Instead it leans unequivocally to the west, to the American cultural impulse. In this way we lean towards the ahrimanic, and not towards the luciferic impulse.

This deviation from Europe's real goal has a direct effect on humanity's health in Europe and of course on the rest, especially on the western world. The illnesses which the people of the west must increasingly fight against and which are *not* of a karmic nature — at least not of an *individual* karmic nature — are directly related to the illness of the social organism, that is, to the unrealized spiritual and Christian-moral goals of today's civilization. The overuse of our lower senses is not the least of the contributing factors.[18]

5. The Spiritual Causes of Individual and General Human Illnesses

In general we can understand the outbreak of a certain illness in an individual as the expression of a karmic cause. From spiritual science we know that the disposition to the development of an illness reflects the result of certain behaviour, of deeds in a previous life. Nevertheless, we should not ignore the fact that an illness is not sent by the opposing powers. It is we ourselves who really bring it about, but it is the *good divine* spirits who convert our karmic behaviour in a previous life to a special 'task' in the present life in order to give us the opportunity to grow by means of this task. The individual's illness, whether it be the flu or a heart condition, is caused by his moral biography during the previous incarnation. So-called risk factors, which may really precede the illness, merely display the instruments, the 'helpers' that cause the karmic illness to break out in this life, so that a healthy balance in the soul can be attained.[19] Thus an individual destiny-related illness is always also an act of love by the good spirits. Everyone has already experienced how an illness has in a certain sense allowed him to mature, has given him a kind of opportunity in a realm that is entirely different from the physical one. Therefore in an individual illness the karmic background is always involved, and we can well imagine that a successful treatment by the attending doctor requires a correct and appropriate knowledge of the patient's whole nature and of his karmic biography. Anthroposophical medicine attempts to meet these requirements. Such an exhaustive treatment, however, can hardly be performed as long as the spiritual image of man is denied by western and European medicine. An entire culture would have to develop the will to educate itself in this respect.

But there are also illnesses which cannot be explained by the individual's destiny, epidemics for example, illnesses which affect whole groups of people or even nations and potentially involve thousands or millions. If we understand the illness of an individual as a karmic necessity, then the same illness in the *many* must be the result of a *shared* karmic necessity. It is then not a question of an individual destiny, but of a people's or even humanity's destiny. For the karma of humanity, which must be resolved, also exists. (For this reason the person affected by an epidemic is not necessarily directly responsible for its outbreak. As one who has been afflicted, he helps resolve humanity's karma by a sacrifice. It is similar, by the way, with natural catastrophes, in which people who are in no way karmically related suffer the same destiny, the same death.)

Rudolf Steiner indicated that plagues relate to past injustices by a people. They are 'something incomplete, which is moved from within to without'.[20] The injustice with which the western and European peoples burdened themselves during the last generations is that of carrying the materialistic world-view of the nineteenth century on into the twentieth century, instead of spiritualizing their world-view, which would have revealed humanity's historic task at the end of the nineteenth century.

An epidemic or a plague can also affect other components than the physical body, and therefore are not only carried by bacteria or viruses but can also be carried by certain psychological developments, the results of which extend to the 'outer anatomy and physiology'.

In this sense, and if we take seriously Rudolf Steiner's remarks about plagues being the result of past injustices of peoples, then an illness like dementia can also be called a kind of plague. That the western world and its science do not consider dementia to be a plague is the result of their concentration on the physical aspect of health, which has become just as much a materialist science as any other. Claiming that a person becomes ill because he is 'genetically disposed' can only be justified if we bear in mind that a genetically conditioned anomaly indicates a karmic cause, that is, a psycho-spiritual process whereby the genetic disposition is again 'only' the instrument for the illness breaking out. This can apply to an individual's destiny as well as that of an entire people. For — as described above — not only an individual karma exists, but also a people's karma or even humanity's karma.

Quite a few illnesses affecting Europeans today are typically cultural illnesses of the western world, not of the east. Many thousands of people in Europe have been affected by dementia, a development (as a plague) which originated in North America.[21] This is above all the result of the fact that Europe's task has not been grasped, that no balancing out of the predominant ahrimanic impulses has been made. Instead Europe is oriented towards a culture that almost exclusively judges the world according to our lower senses. Therefore Europeans are affected by dementia in epidemic form. And an epidemic or plague doesn't only affect older people. It is the symptom of a human scourge which can affect almost *all* ages. The results of recent research indicate that in fact dementia is already affecting 30 to 40 year-olds, and the changes in brain tissue, which lead to the aggravated symptoms of dementia, have been diagnosed in people who are still in the earlier stages of development.

Rudolf Steiner indicated that a healthy moral impulse, that is, a *spiritual* nature, is to be considered as a basis for a healthy physical, material nature:

> Whoever sees through these things will of course not take them as a reason for opposing modern medicine with its external remedies. But a real improvement will never come about through these external methods. What will come about later always reveals itself in advance through esoteric knowledge. This consists of rightly perceiving how morality in the present can lead to better health in the future.[22]

According to this perspective it is at least justifiable to describe dementia as a human plague, or at least as a sickness of civilization. The concept dementia—'demens', 'without spirit'—describes precisely the current state of our western culture.

When for a period of time such a spiritless culture is practised, eventually it begins to have consequences. The spirit, namely the I, as the organizing and 'tightening' entity of the lower components of being, slowly withdraws from the other components. When this happens the astral body begins to wander about like a 'vagabond'.

Those who live or interact with people afflicted with dementia will have experienced what this means. The relatives and friends of a dementia afflicted person can experience how the personality changes, as if he is no longer 'master in his own home'. The aspect of feeling forges ahead; sometimes expressions or impulses break out which were previously unknown. If we again consider this process from a viewpoint reflecting knowledge of man, we realize that this transformation is attributable to the fact that the I, the highest component of being, no longer fully controls the lower components, the soul for example, because it has become weak and is gradually withdrawing from the body.

The consciousness of the memory-representations recorded in the etheric body, which occur in old age, now occurs through the astral body. A representation, when retrieved from memory, releases a feeling. The representation itself, however, is no longer processed by the I, and is immediately forgotten. But the feeling which the memory released does not immediately vanish because, in contrast to the memory-representations, feelings are *persistent*. The astral body remains active. Therefore the representations that have not been made conscious owing to the withdrawal of the I-organization, appear in the form of behaviour laden with feelings, which, because they derive from the affected person's subjective representations, can seem irrational to others. In the most advanced stages of dementia, however, even the feelings come to a standstill, because the astral body also begins to withdraw from the rest of the bodily organization.[23]

Rudolf Steiner explained that during the thinking process destruction of matter in the human head takes place by which the etheric is made free, in the course of which the representations become conscious. The etheric is also separated in the sensory organs during the process of perceiving. If there is a disturbance in this process, as is the case with dementia, we can think of it in the following way. The etheric can then *not* be separated during sensory perception, whereupon the person is unable to be conscious of his representations. This can lead to a persecution complex, for example, something that happens frequently to people with dementia, because unconscious representations which do not correspond to reality erupt without control.[24]

In addition, Rudolf Steiner indicated that with sensory perception, matter in us is removed. We should imagine this process concretely. As soon as we indulge in a sensory perception, in the origin of which the I participates, physical substance in us is degraded, destroyed. Thus something like 'holes' arises, which leads to a feeling of hunger.[25] But the person can refill the cavity created by the destruction of matter by means of his thinking. Dedication to the senses and the allures of the sensory world, which lead to the *destruction of matter*, is caused by the intervention of the *luciferic* powers. The mere processing of the sensory perceptions, which Rudolf Steiner often also called 'dead' thinking, creates a *compression* of matter, a materialization, and is the result of the intervention of *Ahriman* (according to Rudolf Steiner).[26]

Metaphorically speaking, we continually plug up the holes caused by luciferic intervention with dead thoughts, which brings about a materialization, which is an ahrimanic intervention.

Humanity could exist forever in this way if it did not find itself in a slow, but inexorable process of physical degeneration, as mentioned above. It is therefore also necessary to have 'living' creative thoughts apart from the 'dead' ones, in order that the physical in man can become spiritualized and continue to be useful as an instrument.

To briefly outline the three spiritual impulses once again, we first place Lucifer's impulse in opposition to Ahriman's, and finally the redemptive principle, the Christ-impulse, between them:

Lucifer:	Christ:	Ahriman:
Destruction of matter	Livening/spiritualization of matter (the resurrected Body of Christ, which arose from the tomb on Easter morning, was woven of spiritualized matter)	Accumulation of matter

The processes of destruction of matter and accumulation of matter are held in the normal state of balance by the balancing force of the I. Only when the I can no longer ensure the equilibrium of taking and giving, one of the principles gains the upper hand and the entire process comes to a halt.

6. The Transformation of the 'Invisible' and the 'Visible' Person with Dementia

It has already been ascertained above that dementia is an *ahrimanic* illness and is caused by a hardening of the etheric body. Thus it is plausible that the reception of new sensory impressions—a luciferic process—is barely possible any longer in advanced stages of the illness, until it finally becomes completely impossible. Consequently no 'gaps' or 'holes' to be filled arise in the person. Nevertheless, the filling matter continues to accrue, for 'dead' thinking continues to circulate because no more 'pits' are dug in which the filling matter can be inserted. Due to the elimination of the opposing luciferic process, the ahrimanic process continues unabated. The person unconsciously begins again and again to process old sensory impressions with the astral body, although he had already formed mental pictures (representations) of them, which had long since been stored in the etheric body as memory-representations. Thus the person caught in this ahrimanic process unceasingly accumulates matter by means of his 'dead' thinking, and this mainly happens in the region of the physical body where his thinking takes place, namely in the head. Thus excessive hardening, that is, materialization, impedes the functioning of the brain. The hardening tendency leads first to the death of small, then ever larger parts of the brain, and finally leads to so-called vascular dementia, due to sclerosis.

The excesses in the etheric body and its hardening, which is incurred by dead thinking, can also result in the brain's dissolution. When this stage is reached, not even 'dead' thinking is possible.[27]

We might think that this is a luciferic process, but it is not; this is also an ahrimanic process. But in this case the ahrimanic being is not overly concerned with materializing already existing matter — in this case the brain. The brain *is*, after all, already matter. The ahrimanic being is much more intent on hardening the *spiritual* components, that is, to bring the spiritual in man down to the level of matter. So Ahriman works on the etheric body to cause it to harden. But when the etheric body, which is responsible for vivifying the organs, is hardened, the physical-material element in the human being dissolves. This is called neuro-degenerative dementia.

Thus the dying out of portions of the brain is not the cause of memory or thinking loss, but it is a result of the enlarging and simultaneous hardening of the etheric body in the head.

It would seem to be an ironic twist of destiny which the western world itself has brought about. In a culture in which preserving the physical body (which is now understood as the entire human being as such) is the highest goal, less interest in one's fellow men is cultivated; in a culture in which material values have priority over Christian ethics, we strive with all possible means to keep our own material bodies alive as long as possible. But as a result of this conduct the physical body is subject to all manner of diseases, and so for a long period of time, perhaps half of its life, it is ailing. The spirit, which this culture has declared to be nonexistent, actually no longer vivifies the physical body. Matter rapidly degenerates because it is no longer vivified by the spirit.

Rudolf Steiner also indicated that dead thinking, which today especially dominates western civilization, is really a subtle sense of smell. So when the westerner sees the world today, that is, when he ponders the world with the lower senses, he is using his sense of smell rather than his sense of thought:

> ... for modern anatomy and physiology have already discovered, or at any rate have a well-founded hypothesis, that modern thinking really has its roots in the sense of smell, that thinking is bound up with the brain — thus not at all with the higher senses, but with a metamorphosis of the sense of smell. This characteristic attitude of ours in our grasp of the outer world is quite different from the relationship that Plato had. It is not a product of the higher senses; it is a product of the sense of smell, if I may put it so. I mean that today our perfection as humans does not come from our having developed the higher senses, but from our having created for ourselves a modified, meta-morphosed dog's muzzle. This peculiar way of relating ourselves to the outer world is quite different from the way which befits a spiritual epoch.[28]

From this we can conclude that a person who lives and understands the world mostly with his lower senses must find his related thinking paralysed once he loses his sense of smell. It is surely not a higher thinking that such a person exercises when using his lower senses, but it is characteristic today, and when he loses it he is categorized as no longer socially viable.

The most recent research into Alzheimer's disease has shown that one of the first symptoms of its onset is loss of the sense of smell. This characterizes and confirms the kind of sensory perception, and at least indirectly the resulting kind of thinking, which dominates in our western culture—as Rudolf Steiner described over 80 years ago.

Without doubt the enlivenment of our culture by spiritualized thinking, as for example through the anthroposophical path of spiritual training or the preliminary stage which leads to it, the study of spiritual-scientific ideas, would have a strong effect on the prevalence of dementia. For if spiritually living thinking were to replace sensory thinking, man's etheric component would not harden; his body would not become sclerotic, but spiritualized. A better understanding of the threefold (body-soul-spirit) human nature would have healing effects on the social organism and would lead to a fundamental improvement in the area of medicine, curative education and nursing—to the point where 'culturally determined' illnesses such as dementia would recede.

7. 'Dead' and 'Living' Remembering

Just as 'dead thinking' exists, there is also such a thing as 'dead remembering'. The use of mental pictures, or representations, is its antithesis. The transformation of what is remembered into imaginative representations is the first stage to 'living remembrance', which is not located in the head, but in the larynx. In the course of its gradual transformation, humanity is also able to develop imaginative vision. This can be observed especially in the youngest generation, and phenomena such as the so-called Attention Deficit Disorder (ADD), although not recognized as such, can indicate the natural development of humanity towards imaginative vision.[29]

Since the beginning of the twentieth century individual cases have been occurring which bring about the gradual development of new spiritual capacities. It is only a question of bringing these 'living' remembrances to consciousness whether the human being can use them as the foundation for new self-knowledge, or if he will only be troubled by them. An example of a 'living' remembrance – one that does not lose precision by the recalling – is the memory of a previous incarnation. The memory's quality is completely different from the usual one, and that it is more precise is due to it having been clarified by the post-mortem retrospection of the experiences in the previous incarnation and by all the succeeding events in the life between death and rebirth. The remembrance is thus free of all representations which deviate from the reality of what actually occurred. It is, to be precise, not a memory-representation but a pure remembrance. (In the case of such a living remembrance, the person, for the reasons described, is even able to remember the once personal bias of his ideas about the events in a previous life, and be conscious that they really *were* biased and how they differed from the real events.)

'Living' remembering is a gift of the present Michael age, in which the human being begins to develop spiritual organs for the visioning of the Christ Being in etheric form. During sleep, a large part of humanity perceives the appearance of the etheric Christ, but in the waking state, or in an elevated spiritual state, this (still) seldom occurs. Sleep is an unconscious looking inwards; *living* remembering is a conscious looking inwards.

With imaginative or 'spiritual' vision, whether consciously in meditation, for example, or unconsciously in sleep, we have a different perception of our surroundings than with sensory vision. The I senses the function of what in spiritual science is called the Guardian of the Threshold, through which it is protected from the disorientation which inevitably occurs when it becomes aware of the differences between the spiritual and the sensory worlds. The I ensures a cautious confrontation with the spiritual realities which, when observing the sensory world alone, cannot be realized.

But it is just in people who have dementia that the I is no longer able to take over this function of the Guardian. It is weak in relation to the other components of being. The I withdraws more and more from the lower components, until the astral body gives free rein to all that the I had been keeping under control. The person also loses the protection provided by the Guardian of the Threshold, so that he is helplessly exposed to the disparate experiences of the spiritual and sensory worlds. The increasing lack of orientation in respect to the environment in dementia is the result of the lack of orientation about the differences between the concepts of space and time in the sensory and spiritual worlds, and also about the difference between 'dead remembering' of the stored sense perceptions of present life and the unconscious 'living remembrances' – without the I's guidance – such as those of previous incarnations.

This process is Ahriman's great plan, or that of even higher dark powers, to prevent the human being from envisioning the Christ Being in the etheric world that surrounds and permeates our sensory world, and to utilize this envisioning as a foundation for spiritual and physical development. It is truly an antichristian struggle against humanity's general awakening to living remembrance. In this way Ahriman tries with every means to take away man's conscious control of his remembering process. He uses our comfortable materialistic thinking for this. But materialistic thinking is only the instrument for carrying out Ahriman's plan to prevent humanity from achieving wholly conscious living remembrance, and he possesses an ice-cold, genial ability, added to the previously described processes which are responsible for the dementia phenomenon. They are all means helping to carry out this antichristian plan in the realm of matter, one coming from the spiritual world that works into the sensory world.

We can understand why the forming of living remembrance — that of imaginative representations which are neither sensory nor desire-filled mental images — should be prevented by Ahriman by an excessive storing of 'dead' memories in the etheric body, as was described previously. The halt in removing encrusted memory representations prevents new, living processes from arising. (We should take these processes into account in interpersonal relations with the patient as well as his living space. Arranging an environment which corresponds to what he is accustomed, or even to preserve his present spatial situation, for someone who can barely digest new impressions because he is stuck in his hardened etheric body only alleviates the problem for a short time, or seems to do so. In reality, by exclusively accumulating the familiar objects or situations, the repeated looking at old photo albums or such things, only strengthens or accelerates the process of etheric body hardening.)

By exposing this ahrimanic plan and process we can at least begin to understand how dementia originates. It is predisposed in early years by the worsening developments in the social organism, as described earlier. In western countries, where dementia is especially prevalent, people are ever less able to continue their spiritual development into old age. Although through allopathic medicinal achievements people are living longer, they are less wise. It is not really a problem of a younger generation lacking in respect, and which no longer wants to be oriented by the older generation. The attitude of the younger generation is a natural reaction to the fact that the wisdom which old people possessed in the past is no longer present in most older people. If then in later years an attack on the I takes place and dementia occurs, the person stands there without wisdom, without inner equilibrium and peace, something which *natural* old-age forgetfulness could balance out.

8. Where Does the Spirit of the Person with Dementia Go and How Can They be Helped?

Now the I is without its wise higher guidance, which we could also call the higher I residing in the spiritual world. It does not wish to let itself be damaged by the ahrimanic attack and therefore withdraws more and more from the dementia patient's physical organization. For the person affected by dementia this seems to be a vicious circle, for once the withdrawal of the I — as the result of ahrimanic influences — has begun, the withdrawal becomes more intense, although as a consequence of a redemptive intervention. The I bids farewell to the present incarnation and passes over into a kind of sleeping consciousness. But because of this an astral body lacking orientation remains on earth. This alone would not be dangerous for the person involved, were his soul and body not exposed to the danger of other powers taking possession of him.

For this reason, another individual with morally pure intentions must take over the I-function of the sick person. Because of the I's absence, actions and reactions reminiscent of a young child's behaviour occur.[30]

In the small child the I is not yet independently adapted to the processes of life and consciousness. The I-forces of the mother substitute for the natural temporary absence of the I-organization. The dementia patient also needs this kind of care, although it must be taken into account that his astral body, in contrast to that of a small child, is replete with unpurified drives and desires which, depending on life changes and karmic preconditions, can unleash serious problems. The patient can only be brought to a certain inner tranquility and to a relative equilibrium if the carer is fully conscious of the task of providing an organizing I-force for the patient. This is hard work, for one's own astral impulses must always be controlled and dominated during involvement with the sick person. This is also applicable to caring relatives and friends who have only occasional contact with the patient. In the presence of someone afflicted with dementia, one must try to keep one's own psychological inconsistencies to a minimum and maintain an inner equilibrium. Caring for a dementia patient is therefore a truly Christian deed, which is in diametric and thereby healing opposition to the causes of the illness, namely the unchristian elements in today's social organism.

It must always be taken into account that the brain is not the real problem with dementia; rather it is the deferral or blocking of the components of being's* tasks. If we were to think of the brain isolated from the components of being it would be as if we expected that the head could function 'unattached', isolated from the body.

Taking over the I-function by another person should also be reflected in the living environment and in the programme for a residential caring institute.

---

*Meaning the physical body, etheric body, astral body and the I.

The afflicted person's I is usually no longer embracing the lower components of being, but has spread out to more distant regions. Therefore it cannot pass on the sensory impressions to the body, embracing them. So we should attempt to design rooms that allow the I to move in a kind of rotation, meaning that the I learns to limit itself and find its way homeward to the patient's body, where it can tend to the processing or to the conscious absorption of the sensory impressions. The I would then enter into a spiralling movement similar to the zodiac sign of Cancer.

If this form were used in a living-space programme, it would take the components of being problematic into consideration and help to alleviate the progressive hardening of the etheric body. Round or circular forms, and also interlinking curves, such as those of snail or nautilus shells, would support this embracing process – the beneficial encircling of the patient's physical organization by the I and the astral body.

A living-space concept that takes the causes of the illness into consideration and is attuned to its development would have to include these elements.

It would have to be organized according to the

concept of 'assisted living', which provides for the carer to live in the same house as the patient. This arrangement is not only important because of the effort involved in the amount of care necessary in advanced stages of the illness; it is also necessary because the patient must be cared for by someone who provides his or her I-forces. We could also imagine, if necessary, an arrangement in which the carer comes to the patient in shifts, which of course would compromise the assisted living concept. It is also doubtful if such a responsible task as providing one's own I-function to another person is practicable in the rhythm of shift-work. The carers would then be virtually leading two lives: one at home and the other in the institute providing care. Only in the rarest of cases could it be implemented without resulting in a stressful situation for the patient as well as for the carer.

It seems that the caring for a dementia patient is a very expensive undertaking, and not only because of the exterior conditions, such as the expense of the care provision itself, but also because of the spiritual and anthropological nature of the illness. Carers would have to be found who consider it their life's mission and their destiny's vocation to be constantly together, at least during a part of their lives, with one, two or three dementia patients, and not as a passing fulfilment of duty in a stressful job. This can only happen out of real love, as a sacrifice not accompanied by inner discord. During the candidates' interviews it would have to be decidedly emphasized that only people with this attitude be accepted in the assisted living plan.[31]

We could think of this as an irony of destiny that humanity has brought upon itself through the propagation of an egoism so far unknown in an age when, according to Rudolf Steiner, the evolution of a once necessary materialism should be brought to an end and be replaced by an active spiritual life imbued with Christian morality—ironic because humanity is not able to purify its own conduct. And because of the stimulus of an increasingly egoistical culture, very few people will be found who are willing to perform this kind of care-giving service. A huge predominance of those needing care over carers is already evident. The egoism of the western world has created this epidemic. Now the western world is itself affected by this epidemic, and because it lacks the Christian impulse it is clueless as to how to remedy it.

The result of this cluelessness is not only pushing back old age—a paradox considering that the young also want to live as long as possible—but the desire to live long is not accompanied by an understanding of the ageing process and its consequences. (Today we dare not become 'old', at most 'older', but in any case keep 'fit'.) Another consequence is the generation of egoistical, materialistic ideas, such as so-called assisted suicide, which hinders the fulfilment of karmic necessities and simultaneously attests to an unusual type of humanitarianism. Thus the western world must suffer the consequences of its mental and moral conduct. We have raised our children in egoism and must now reckon with the situation that when we become ill because of our egoism we are not looked after by them; for they have grown into an implicit egoism, because their I has not been cultivated, and because they are weak and are without sufficient strength to perform a Christian sacrifice of love. But such Christian acts of love constitute the only effective help in cases of sickness. And only with a certain spiritual grounding in knowledge about the real causes of dementia, as well as about man as a being of various components, should a person lend his I-forces to another.

A concept such as is found in many curative education institutes is therefore advisable. However, we should always be aware that dementia patients suffer from an ahrimanic illness, and are not like most children in need of special care who carry within them unused, pure childhood energy. Instead, they are people who have been affected by life, who at the point in their lives when the strongest I-forces should have been developed have completely withdrawn; and also their astral bodies have been filled up and burdened during a long life. A person whose lower components of being have collected all kinds of uncontrolled representations and tramp about like 'vagabonds' needs the strong I-forces of a carer nearby. Therefore children, especially small ones, should not be integrated in a care-giving programme for dementia patients, as opposed to what is the case in a curative education institute. Handicapped children can mature psychologically from contact with the non-handicapped ones, as well as the non-handicapped from the handicapped, for the I-development of the non-handicapped is wonderfully stimulated in company with those in need of soul-care.

In the case of dementia patients, however, children

living in the same place would be burdened, and they can hardly help, because their own I is not yet fully awake and they are still dependent on the I-forces of their educators.

For this reason it is advisable not to accept carers under 21 years of age, for the protection of their own development and because they are not mature enough for the demanding task, and are thus not able to dedicate enough I-forces to it without hurting themselves. People with experience of life, a strong I and the above-described grounding in knowledge are needed.

Nor is the integration of a dementia section in an existing ordinary geriatric institution advisable. Neither the normal residents nor the dementia afflicted would benefit from such an arrangement. It would only result in a confusing situation for both.

In order to more effectively recall the vanishing I-forces of the dementia patient back to the lower components and thereby mitigate their hardening, all the increasingly utilized peripheral activities — 'therapies' — such as television and loud electronic music should be prohibited. Instead means should be utilized which direct the I back to other people, such as practising and then observing the art of sculptural modelling, which induces the integration of the I with the astral body, for the astral body is called upon to grasp the spatial forms, and the I to transform the spatial perceptions into living representations. The etheric body, however, is more attuned to creative drawing activities. Painting should also at first play an active, then a passive role. In the stages of the illness which are not yet very advanced, dramatics may also be practised, which encourages the energizing of the I-force, by acting as well as by watching.

What perspective is in store for a social organism which in the near future could consist of a quarter or even a third of its people without an active I-function? The anthroposophical viewpoint can offer the following answer. Humanity would be ill-advised to doubt the considerable impact of the ahrimanic forces. Even if the causes of the dementia epidemic are the result of an ahrimanic cultural life, it can also offer the opportunity for the spiritualization of humanity. Thus in a culture influenced by Ahriman, the Christian forces of compassion, endurance and love, although scarce, can be lighted anew. For it has been shown already how, in company with the person afflicted with dementia, these attributes of the carer lead to very beneficial effects — for the ill person as well as for the carer. This moral attitude would not only have a positive influence on the following generation and lead to a certain implicitness in care-giving work, but the prevalence of the illness itself would be limited from the outset by such a standard. Thus from an evil a good could arise — Mephistopheles in Goethe's *Faust*: 'I am a part of that force that always wants evil, and always creates the good'[32] — which can bring humanity a step further in its long and arduous path to becoming gods through the impulse of Christ.[33]

Notes

GA = *Gesamtausgabe* or Collected Works of Rudolf Steiner. For a list of translated editions, see page 77.

1. See Rudolf Steiner, *How to Know Higher Worlds*, Anthroposophic Press (GA 10).
2. The 'I' should not to be confused with the 'ego'. What the ego attempts, in contrast to the I, is to make one's own drives and wishes prevail. It is completely concentrated on itself and not on the world and on the other person. In fact, the ego is our unpurified astral body. The I should dominate this ego, and not the contrary — the ego should not dominate the I.
3. Prof. Hubert Markl, former president of the Max Planck Institute, in *Der Spiegel*, 15 December 2000: 'The popular arguments in philosophical and para-philosophical debate about what is "natural" and "unnatural" often lack a sound basis. For example, it is claimed that a person not originated by a randomly determined gene-lottery would lose his freedom and therewith a substantial part of his human dignity...'
4. John, 11:25.
5. If the human being were really from a 'randomly determined gene-lottery', then it is statistically very surprising, considering how different individuals are, that a very passable, 'meaningful' result should come about. Apart from the fact that no randomness could be responsible for billions of unique, artistically endowed or, prosaically expressed, 'properly functioning' people, we cannot accept this statement as credible, for man would then be the product of pure chance.

6. In many lectures, Rudolf Steiner presented a clear picture of the direct relation between the physical and spiritual make-up of the human being, above all in his *Study of Man* and *Occult Physiology* and also in his teachings about the senses. Rudolf Steiner's complex works cannot be the subject of this book. However, they are essential for an understanding of the human being and his pathological transformations as they take place in, for example, dementia.

7. In Rudolf Steiner we find little mention of the different ways of recording representations according to their different origins. One of his statements that is helpful in this respect is found in GA 156, p. 116: 'Just as the world with its events is continually recorded in our etheric bodies, we also record in our etheric bodies what we ourselves experience psychologically.' Here two different kinds of recordings are differentiated. 'We know that representations are remembered in different ways, depending on how long ago they arose. [...] In any case, what is experienced as a representation attached to a sensory impression is brought into the stream of time in which we ourselves live. [...] The memory is also at one with the etheric body, the representations with the astral body and sensory impressions with the I.' (GA 206, p. 122) From this it can be seen that a representation which did *not* derive from a sensory impression does not have contact with the I in the same way as a representation acquired through the I—although both kinds of representation come about through the activity of the astral body. As long as an astral body not fully integrated with the I remains in contact with the person's representations, they will always be reflections of what is personal. If memory-representations are only formed from what is happening externally, they never correspond exactly

with what is really happening there. But when representations are remembered which arise independently of a sensory impression, they are as a rule even less exact than the memory-representations of sensory events.

8. Rudolf Steiner (GA 115, p. 199).

9. In every representation the I is present at least to a certain extent. However, there is a difference between an activity of the I which is unconscious or subconscious and one guided by the I-consciousness.

10. 'When spontaneous movements [of the physical body] occur, that is, of an innocent kind, then anyone who considers such things can see that in a certain category of spontaneous movements after effects of experiences remain.' (GA 206, p. 124)

11. The result of practising the retrospection exercise with the force of consciousness—a 'nurtured' memory-tableau—can also, incidentally, provide for an easier orientation in the spiritual world after crossing the threshold.

12. Jacques Lusseyran indicated how the astral body can be cleansed nightly from impurities or 'pollution'. See: Jacques Lusseyran, *And there was Light,* and *Against the Pollution of the I.*

13. 'A clear proof of the fact that human beings today are only at home when it comes to a mechanical way of thinking that can always determine whether things have been rightly or wrongly thought out, and which celebrates the brilliant triumphs it has produced for modern civilization—a proof of this is that humanity today has confidence only in mechanical thinking, which immediately shows how nonsensical it is when applied to fields other than mechanics. Everything, the nature of the world and its organisms, should be mechanical concepts today, because we

still only have trust in mechanical thinking.' (GA 310, p. 11)

14. With more or less strong deviations from this age.

15. The word 'dilutes' does not refer to a material activity of the etheric body, which obviously cannot apply to it as a spiritual component. It is rather a metaphor for a purely spiritual process, which, however, has an effect on the physical body.

16. In the case of uncontrolled motor activity in a dementia patient, it can be caused by the fact that '... what has been experienced is too strongly impressed in the physical body; it may still be impressed in the etheric body, but not too strongly in the physical body. If it is impressed too strongly in the physical body, then this physical body comes under the influence of the remembrances. That it should not do.' (GA 206, p. 124)

This must be distinguished from the normal, healthy impressing of experiences in the physical body, which, the older a person becomes, can be read in his physiognomy or posture: 'We cannot say that the physical body is the carrier of memory; that is the etheric body. But for us human beings what remains in the etheric body of our thought would slip away in the physical body, as dreams slip away when they cannot be engraved in the physical matter of the physical body.' (GA 167, page 31) 'When in later life we remember something from earlier experiences, it means that we stamp the astral body, which then unites with the etheric body, with what has remained in our physical body as an imprint, like the impression of a seal.' (GA 159, p. 144.)

17. 'Aristotle's compilation of abstract logic was the first milestone on the path of this de-spiritualization of human soul-life [...] of taste, sense of smell, sense of balance, sense of movement, sense of life, sense of

touch = occidental culture (lower man). And now a civilization began that was based essentially upon these senses. Even if you do not at first admit it, nevertheless it is so. For take the scientific spirit that has emerged, the scientific spirit that tries to apply mathematics to everything. But mathematics [...] comes from the senses of movement and of balance. Thus even the most spiritual things discovered by modern science come from the lower man. Of course people talk about seeing, or about the eye, or about the sense of sight; but one who sees through these things knows that all the concepts that are used are somehow conjured from the sense of touch to the sense of sight. People do not notice it, but in describing the sense of sight they make use of categories, of ideas, which apply to the sense of touch.' (GA 206, Dornach, pp. 34f.)

18. Presently it is generally assumed that humanity has always suffered from the phenomenon of dementia. But it was not diagnosed or identified as such, mostly because life expectancy in earlier times was much shorter than it is now. However, the shorter life expectancy in previous centuries was also due to the higher death rate of infants and children. Furthermore such grave impediments in old age such as memory loss, use of speech and motor activity as appear typically in dementia are not found very much in historical sources. In contrast, in earlier centuries it was a matter of course to ask advice from the elderly who, because of their wisdom enjoyed great social esteem, whereas today the external process of ageing is felt to be a stigma, which is to be avoided by all manner of methods, from fitness training to plastic surgery, in order not to be branded by society as 'functionally inept' and therefore ignored. Here the paradox of the western world-view is made obvious by its own logic:

because only life limited to the physical-material sensory world can be imagined, the desperately striven for goal is to preserve the physical-material component as long as possible. (Because the spiritual in man is denied, the physical-material component is more and more seen as the entire human being.) By means of such methods life expectancy in most 'civilized' countries, above all in the west, has increased enormously. But this increase, induced by the fear of departing from the physical-material world, conflicts with the naturally declining process of the human physical-material component. A life, up to two-thirds of which proceeds with the visible signs of the inexorable process of decline is, for all materialistic thinking souls, the bitter consequence of their original goal of 'eternal' physical-material life. That the concept dementia (from *de-mens* = without/away from spirit) has been used by physicians only since the nineteenth century shows that this illness has appeared so seldom that it wasn't felt necessary to find a name for it. It was only in the twentieth century that there has been serious scientific research about what is known to us today as dementia.

19. The relation between a way of life in a previous incarnation and a certain illness is that of a disposition for it. The person is therefore not helplessly given up to it, for it doesn't necessarily have to break out. By the way he leads his life, or because of other factors from without which influence his development, the outbreak of a karmic illness can be avoided.

20. GA 93a, page 73.

21. The tremendous outbreak of dementia nowadays has its causes in human thinking as it has developed mainly in western civilization, especially since the beginning of the age of Michael. What is *not* meant here

is that 'the North American people' as such are branded as the cause of the dementia plague, but only that the way of thinking is described as being different from that of the eastern peoples.

22. GA 93a, page 234.

23. The terrifying expression 'vegetating away' has a certain justification in this stage of the illness, which is more or less limited to a physical-etheric existence.

24. Here it is not a question of becoming conscious of previously unconsciously processed representations, but the elevation of what the withdrawing I once kept locked in the depths of the astral and etheric bodies.

25. Compare GA 67, p. 343.

26. See GA 67, lectures on 13 and 14 August 1921, p. 158, GA 217, p. 47 and GA 83, p. 320.

27. In so-called vascular dementia the hardening process of the etheric body in the physical body is so advanced that it leads to chronic arteriosclerosis in the area of the head. The blood, which is the physical carrier of the I, can no longer reach the head. In neurodegenerative dementia, such as Alzheimer's disease, the enlarging and hardening of the etheric body in the head region causes the dying out of the brain cells.

28. GA 206, p. 35.

29. What children see or experience with their new supersensible capacities conflicts with the viewpoints of many teachers and other adults. The child is, in a manner of speaking, obliged to live in a world which does not correspond to its necessities. This necessarily leads to abnormal behaviour. (This behaviour surely does not apply to all children who are so diagnosed. Although modern medicine and behaviour research tend to contrive ever more complicated and diverse categories for classifying children, it seems that the generic label ADD is much too frequently applied to all

those children who display behavioural problems because of many diverse reasons, or whose behaviour is not considered adequate according to current ideas. Many such behavioural problems are the result of the increasing denial of the human being's spiritual origin in his education. In the child's soul this can cause damage which is extremely difficult to repair, because such educational methods cannot be brought into agreement with his soul's own experiences. And through such methods the I, trying to integrate with the physical and spiritual components of being, is continuously pushed away.)

30. This 'absence' of the I is most noticeable in close relations with the affected person. Relatives often have the impression that he is no longer 'at home', that the real person whom they had known for many years is simply no longer there.

31. In this respect, pedagogical institutes would have to be established in which the prospective caregivers have at least a basic experience in general and spiritual-scientific knowledge of the human being.

32. J.W. von Goethe, *Faust*, Part 1, 'In the Study'.

33. 'By means of the normal earthly human forces, I take from the earth everything which the earth gives me for my I. When I look at the Mystery of Golgotha, I assimilate something which takes me away from this earth, which kindles in me a life that otherwise could not have been kindled. By my inclination towards the Mystery of Golgotha I assimilate something supersensible. I realize that humanity must have a new kind of supersensible inner feeling and cognition, as opposed to the old way when humanity still experienced living thinking, that man shall receive such an understanding from the Mystery of Golgotha through which he becomes aware of his own dead thinking,

and that he consciously enters into supersensible existence, so that he can say: Not I, but Christ in me makes me alive after the Mystery of Golgotha.

In order that the human being can say that, modern initiation science, modern anthroposophy, can provide the vital stimulus. Because we receive this stimulus through modern initiation science, we will see emerge from it not an anti-religious life but a deepened religious life in that we consciously deviate from what has come to us from the past. And through spiritual-scientific knowledge the human being will be led away from all the doubts which are so strongly contained today in religious life and in the teachings of natural science which, nevertheless, had made us free people. On the one hand it has achieved great triumphs, which, on the other hand, has planted understandable doubts in the soul of man about his religious feelings and about knowledge of his supersensible nature. Anthroposophy sets itself the task of sweeping away the strongest doubts from the human soul and nature, which can only be introduced there by natural science, for anthroposophical spiritual science, directly derived from the spirit of science, is to overcome what natural science is not able to overcome. This anthroposophical science will be able to plant true religious life again in the human soul. It will not contribute to killing religious meaning, but it can add to human development to the extent that humanity acquires a new relationship to Christianity through its approach to the Mystery of Golgotha, which can only be understood and accepted through anthroposophy.' (GA 211, p. 176)

Bibliography

Books by Rudolf Steiner

GA/CW (*Gesamtausgabe*/Collected Works)

10   *Knowledge of the Higher Worlds/How to Know Higher Worlds*

67   *Das Ewige in der Menschenseele*

83   *The Tension Between East and West*

93ª   *The Foundation of Esotericism*

115   *A Psycholgy of Body, Soul and Spirit*

156   *Inner Reading and Inner Hearing*

159/60 *Wesen und Bedeutung Mitteleuropas und die europäischen Volksgeister*

167   *Gegenwärtiges und Vergangenes im Menschengeiste*

206   *Menschenwerden, Weltenseele und Weltengeist – Zweiter Teil*

211   *The Sun Mystery and the Mystery of Death and Resurrection*

217   *Becoming the Archangel Michael's Companions*

310   *Human Values in Education*

English titles available from Rudolf Steiner Press, UK: www.rudolfsteinerpress.com or SteinerBooks, USA: www.steinerbooks.org